C is for Cocoa

An Alphabet Book about Ghana, West Africa,
and the food, plants, and animals in its environment

© 2014

By Caroline Brewer, Kimmoly Rice-Ogletree,
and Madam Victoria and Her Third Grade Students
at Timber Junction-Nkwanta School in Konko Village

For more information about the book, contact Caroline Brewer, Unchained Spirit Enterprises at
caroline.unchained@gmail.com or caroline@happyteachertraining.com
or check out the website www.happyteachertraining.com

Dedication & Acknowledgments

This book is dedicated to the precious children of the Timber Junction-Nkwanta School in Konko Village, in the Eastern Region of Ghana.

We were delighted and honored to meet all of the children who attend the school and could not be more grateful for the two days we spent with Madam Victoria Gyinaku and her third grade students. She and they welcomed us into their classroom and showered us with the deepest affection, patience, kindness, and generosity. We thoroughly enjoyed every moment we spent with them. This book is infused with their kind-hearted, creative genius and is being published only because they made it possible.

We warmly extend our gratitude to Washington, D.C. Businesswoman Juanita Britton (Queen Mother of Konko Village) for inviting us as members of Leap for Ghana to the village. We also want to express our deepest thanks to Author and LEAP for Ghana Founder Kwame Alexander and LEAP for Ghana Director Tracy Chiles McGhee for leading us on such an extraordinary journey throughout the Accra Region of Ghana and into the hearts of the people of Konko. We will always remember the gifts of love Konko residents and the people of Ghana bestowed upon us. It was our first trip to the Motherland and we were changed in all ways wonderful as a result.

We offer a very special thank you to Obodai, Nii Obaka, Nii Sai, and Nii Soja Torto for helping us out in a pinch and making an extraordinary effort to take the gorgeous photo for this book that showcases Ghana's chocolate products. The children handled the experience like pros, and their father was exceptionally kind and thoughtful in going the extra mile to deliver exactly what we needed.

We thank all of you who are reading and sharing this book and supporting our humanitarian work with your contributions. You are making dreams come true for us and for more children and families than we ever could count!

Blessings,
Caroline Brewer and Kimmoly Rice-Ogletree

THIRD GRADE STUDENTS OF TIMBER JUNCTION-NKWANTA SCHOOL, KONKO VILLAGE

*Prince Aboyagye * James Odame Adu * Gideon Avaga * Wisdom Avaga * Johnson Afatonu * Gideon Ayesu * Mattew Dormor * Jennifer Adiku * Sistofe Atileh * Akosua Avaga * Kwayisi Abigail Obiribea*

ABOUT THE AUTHORS

Caroline Brewer is an international education consultant and author of 10 books, who has made presentations, including professional development training, to nearly 25,000 teachers, students, parents, and librarians, including at the Indiana Department of Education, and at the Accra, Ghana Region's first Global Literacy Summit. As a newspaper journalist, she served on two Pulitzer Prize juries and was nominated for the prize. Her first Sunday features column was entered into the U.S. Congressional Record.

Kimmoly Rice-Ogletree is President and Founder of the Life Institute for Excellence, LLC, and the Elite Female Mentoring Organization. Mrs. Rice-Ogletree is an entrepreneur, international speaker, published author, and teen success coach. She is an exceptional motivator, full of life and passion. Ms. Rice-Ogletree is the creator of the *Elite Female Mentoring Success Manual, which* offers practical tools to assist teenage girls in reaching their full potential. The curriculum has garnered national attention. It was recently introduced to a Girls Empowerment program in

Madam
Victoria,
3rd Grade
Teacher
at Timber
Junction-
Nkwanta
School,
Konko
Village

Madam Victoria Gyinaku is a
wonderful teacher. We were honored
to work with her during our two days
at the school. She was gracious, kind,
enthusiastic, and generous. We loved
meeting her and working with her
students, who were bright, warm,
kind, and engaging. This book is their
creation.

Top photo- Madam Victoria leads us
and her students on the field trip
through the village to explore the
environment and find food, plants,
and animals that could be included in
this alphabet book.

Bottom Photo – Madam Victoria
shows a terrific, playful spirit as she
follows Caroline in demonstrating the
Mirror Dancing exercise to her
students. Mirror Dancing is a way to
break the ice and allow students and
teachers to release stress and tension,
re-charge, balance both hemispheres
of the brain, and have a good time,
before settling into deeper learning
experiences.

A is for ant
and avocado,
in Mexico
known as
avogato.

B is for bamboo.
B is for bread

and butterflies
soaring overhead.

C is for chocolate, smooth and sweet,

and cocoa,
which makes the treats we eat;

and coconuts on trees 80 feet!

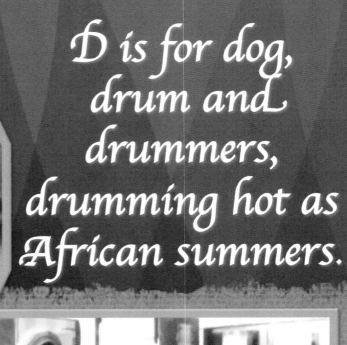

D is for dog,
drum and
drummers,
drumming hot as
African summers.

E is for all of those wobbly eggs,
balanced by magically steady legs.

F is for fish and that fisherman, working long days to catch all he can.

G is for garden egg and gari.
They make dishes yummy and merry.

G is for lumpy ginger that brings
a bit of spice to ev-er-y-thing.

G is for goat,
green peppers,
and grass,
used for
food, drinks,
paper...
Glad you
asked!

H is for hen, mother of chickens.

I is for icy.
I is for ice.
I is jollof,
a tasty rice.

K is for kente.
L is for leaf,

lion and lizard. What a motif!

M is for mango, mountain
and mud. Too much rain
and you get a flash flood!

N is for net.

O is for ocean,
where sand
and water
move
in motion.

O is for onions

and oranges galore!
Straight from the grove.
No need for the store.

P is for palm oil and peppers – hot!
Can you stand a little or – a lot?

P is for pineapple and plantain, growing outward, the way feet extend.

Q is for the Queen, the Queen Mother.
She cares for children like none other.

R is for rainforest, rich with green
tall and long and leafy growing things.

S is for soup and spinach, you see.

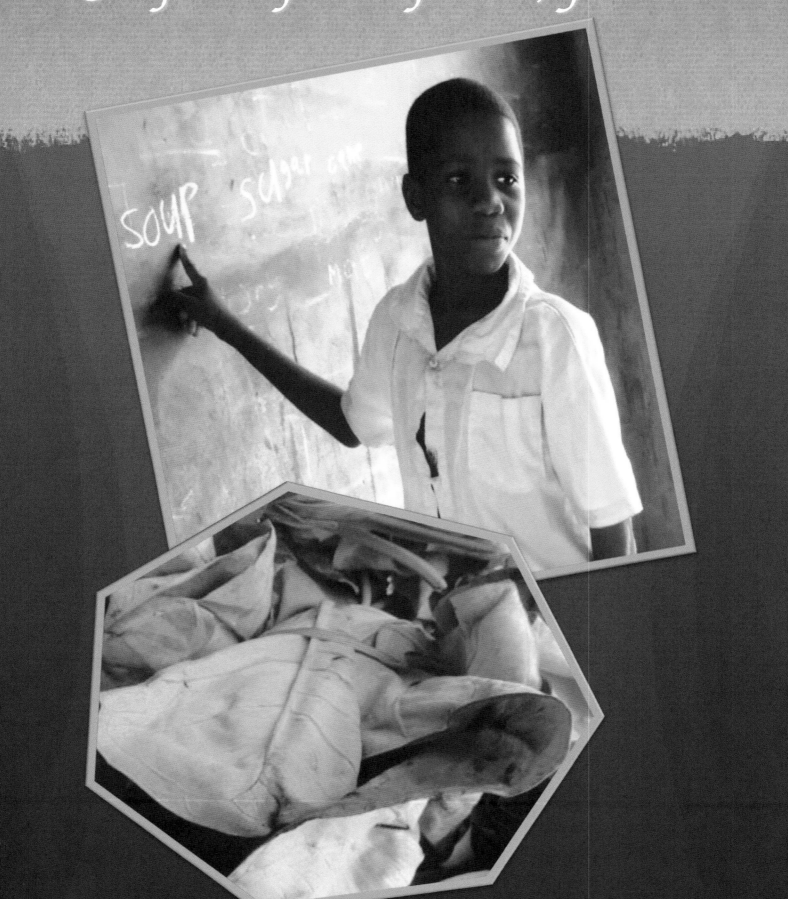

And for sugarcane, nature's candy.

T is for tomatoes and this tree. It has an odd shape. What might it be?

U is for
Ghana's
Umbrella
Tree.
Leaves go
'round
to make
the canopy.

V is for
village

and for vulture, that bird
with the flesh-eating culture.

W is for water, watermelon, and weaver. He weaves yarn into cloth like the busiest beaver.

X is for xylophone, so let's jam!

Y is for yam and more and more yams.

Z is for zebra. This is the end.
Hurry! Come back and read us again!

Madam Victoria, Caroline, Kimmoly & Konko Village Children

C IS FOR COCOA KEY FACTS

Butterfly – Ghana has the only butterfly sanctuary in West Africa. Ghana protects nearly 100 species of butterflies, many (common) to its biologically rich and varied habitat, a paradise for nature lovers. www.ashantiafricantours.com

Chocolate - According to CNN International, "The chocolate industry is worth about $110 billion a year. America consumes the most chocolate of any country, an estimated "764 thousand tons a year." Hershey is the U.S.'s largest chocolate company and largest purchaser of cocoa from West Africa. Chocolate is made from cocoa beans. About 40 cocoa beans are contained in each cocoa pod. One cocoa tree produces about 50 pods twice a year. Each pod has enough cocoa for about eight bars of milk chocolate or four bars of dark. So each tree gives 400-800 bars of chocolate a year. Hawaii is the only state in the U.S. that grows cocoa beans to produce chocolate. *www.edition.cnn.com *www.greenbiz.com/blog *www.chocolateuniversityonline.com *www.divinechocolate.com

Cocoa - Cocoa came to Ghana in 1876 when a Ghanaian named Tetteh Quarshie brought some cocoa pods to Ghana from Equatorial Guinea. By 1911 Ghana was the world's leading cocoa exporter, supplying the growing European chocolate market. Today there are close to 720,000 cocoa farmers in Ghana and approximately 2 million in West Africa. West Africa supplies 70% of the world's cocoa. Ghana is the second largest producer. www.gonetoghana.com

The use of children in farming cocoa is a major problem. According to FairTradeUSA.com, "On hundreds of thousands of cocoa farms, children help out with farming tasks as members of the family, much as they do around the world, for many other crops. At the same time…Surveys in Cote d'Ivoire and Ghana found too many children are performing unsafe farming tasks, and being injured in the process. There are also instances where children may be working instead of attending school, and even moved (or "trafficked") to a farm away from their village, to work full-time. www.fairtradeusa.com

Drum - Known as the oldest instrument in the world, the drum has its place in societies worldwide, but the sacred love and use of the instrument in Africa is unprecedented. Special occasions call for special drums in the African heritage. These drums have more decorations than the average drum and are treated as sacred pieces of art. Most drums in Africa are carved from solid logs of wood or made with several strips of wood bound together by Iron hoops. Drums that are made for children are made from hard fruit shells or discarded tins. Many children in villages view drumming as a way to complete the inner self. Becoming a respected drummer is a sign of maturity in many African cultures, and the few selected to represent their villages are treated as royalty. www.debate.uvm.edu/dreadlibrary/kahn.html

Fishing - The importance of the fisheries sector in the socio-economic development of (Ghana) cannot be overemphasized. With a marine coastline of 550 kilometers stretching from Aflao in the East to Half Assini in the West, the fishing industry plays a major role in sustainable livelihoods and poverty reduction in several households and communities. www.bog.gov.gh

Gari – Gari is the most commercialized cassava product in Ghana and constitutes a daily meal to some 150 million people worldwide. *Gari* (*Garri, Gali*) is made from the tubers of the cassava plant. It is a starchy carbohydrate, used in the same manner as *Rice* and *Couscous* (though gari requires no additional cooking when it is eaten, it only needs to be moistened). Traditionally gari is made at home: cassava tubers are first cleaned, peeled, and soaked in water, they are then grated, and the resulting mass is packed into cotton sacks, topped with weights to squeeze out the water, and allowed to partially dry and ferment for a few days. The grated cassava is then spread out to dry in the sun, pressed through a sieve, and dry-fried in shallow pans until it is completely cooked and free of moisture, and viola! -- gari. The finished gari can be stored until needed. Today, many people in (and out of) Africa use packaged commercially manufactured gari that is sold in shops and markets. www.ghanaweb.com

Kente Cloth - Kente Cloth, (made from cotton, rayon, and silk), is local to Ghana. Kente Cloth there was worn by royalty. It is hand woven in wooden looms and is of very high worth. It comes in a variety of patterns, colors and designs, each of which have different meanings. According to Ghanaian mythology, kente cloth was first created when 2 friends watched how a spider wove its web. By mimicking the actions of the spiders, they created Kente cloth the same way. This story, whether true or not, shows the harmony between Ghanaians and Mother Nature. The Kente cloth is one of the most famous and wanted fabrics in the whole of Africa. For Ghanaians, this cloth represents the history, philosophy, oral literature, religious beliefs, political thought and aesthetic principles of life. www.kentecloth.net

C IS FOR COCOA KEY FACTS

Mountains - **Mount Afadjato** is the highest mountain in Ghana, at an altitude of 885 meters (2,904 ft). The mountain is located in the Agumatsa Range near the villages of Liati Wote and Gbledi, in the Volta Region of Ghana at the border with Togo. en.wikipedia.org/wiki/Mount_Afadjato

Mud houses - In Ghana, traditional houses built of mud provide accommodation for households in villages, small towns and major cities. Mud houses are an important feature of historical urban structures. In Ghana's south, the traditional architectural design of mud houses is rectangular. These structures normally have roofs of iron or aluminum sheets. Mud walls need protection from rain. In Ghana's drier north, most mud buildings are round and have straw roofs. Some houses date back to before 1850…" www.dandc.eu/en/article

Palm Oil - Human use of oil palms may date as far back as 5,000 years…Palm oil from *Elaeis guineensis*…is widely used as a cooking oil. Palm oil formed the basis of soap products, such as Unilever's "Sunlight" soap, and the American Palmolive brand.[22] By around 1870, palm oil constituted the primary export of some West African countries such as Ghana and Nigeria although this was overtaken by cocoa in the 1880s

http://en.wikipedia.org/wiki/Palm_oil

Editor's Note: Some excerpts in the Key Facts Section were edited for space and clarity considerations

Plantain - Ghana is the largest producer of plantain in West Africa and the second in Africa after Uganda and Rwanda (FAO, 2010). Of more than 90% of the cultivated area in the Ghanaian agricultural sector, plantain is ranked third after yam and cassava (FAO, 2010) and contributes about 13.1% to the Agricultural Gross Domestic Product (AGDP). Plantain cultivation is of great socioeconomic importance in Ghana from the viewpoint of food security and job creation. Plantains become abundant on the market from September to March with the peak in December-January. www.thejaps.org.pl/docs

Umbrella Tree (Local Name Odwuma) – A very common tree of the secondary forest, except in drier forests. You can recognise this tree by the leaves, which are big, 50 cm with 8-14 leaflets, arranged in a circle around the top of the petiole, like an umbrella. It has typical big air roots. It even appears along the old logging roads, moving to the forest after disturbance. Common on old farms, but short-lived. It produces a lot of seeds in fruits, which clearly improves the chances that the species will `find' newly exposed gaps in the forest. The wood is used for making canoes. Natural doctors use the leaves to ease stomach problems. www.kakum.ka.funpic.de/trees/03.php

Women carrying baskets on heads - Carrying on the head is common in many parts of the developing world. African-American women continued the practice during the 19th century, which they learned from elder Africans brought from Africa (and enslaved) in America. The practice was efficient, at a time when there were no vehicles available for carrying burdens. Today, women and men may be seen carrying burdens on top of their heads where there is no less expensive, or more efficient, way of transporting workloads. Up to 20% of the person's body weight can be carried with no extra exertion of energy. en.wikipedia.org/wiki/Carrying_on_the_head

Yam – Yams are the staple food of many peoples of western Africa. The yam is a large tuberous root related to the sweet potato, but not exactly the same. American sweet potatoes are usually orange, but African yams can be white, yellow, or orange inside (and come in many shapes and sizes: some can be up to a few feet long). Yams account for 11 percent of total consumption in Ghana in 2007. Ghana is the leading exporter of yam, accounting for over 94 percent of total yam exports in West Africa. www.fao.org (Food and Agriculture Organization of the United Nations - MAFAP) * www.afikpousa.org

Printed in Great Britain
by Amazon